Decorative Fish
Carving

Decorative Fish Carving

Rick Beyer

TAB **TAB BOOKS**
Blue Ridge Summit, PA

Moto-Tool® and Moto-Flex® Emerson Electric Comapny, St Louis, MO

FIRST EDITION
FIRST PRINTING

© 1990 by **TAB BOOKS**
TAB BOOKS is a division of McGraw-Hill, Inc.

Library of Congress Cataloging-in-Publication Data

Beyer, Rick.
    Decorative fish carving / by Rick Beyer.
        p.   cm
    ISBN 0-8306-7568-X   ISBN 0-8306-3568-8 (pbk.)
    1. Wood-carving.   2. Fishes in art.   I. Title.
TT199.7.B49   1990
731.4'62—dc20   90-36461
                                                 CIP

TAB BOOKS offers software for sale. For information and a catalog, please contact TAB Software Department, Blue Ridge Summit, PA 17294-0850.

Questions regarding the content of this book should be addressed to:

Reader Inquiry Branch
TAB BOOKS
Blue Ridge Summit, PA 17294-0214

Acquisitions Editor: Kimberly Tabor
Book Editor: Marie Bongiovanni and Susan L. Rockwell
Production: Katherine G. Brown
Book Design: Jaclyn J. Boone

CONTENTS

FOREWORD

Rick Beyer was born in 1956 in Racine, Wisconsin, where he and his wife Nancy operate their wildlife art gallery.

Rick has spent many hours in the outdoors fishing and enjoying nature. He has vacationed in northern Wisconsin with his family most of his life, fishing whenever possible.

Rick carved his first piece in 1972 at the age of 16. It was a relief carving done on a cross-section of an oak tree, depicting an Irish and an English Setter on point. After this piece, it wasn't until 1980 when he resumed carving. When he began carving again, he created a family of natural finish ducks, then proceeded carving nonstop.

While working as a supervisor for a furniture manufacturer, Rick began specializing in fish. The natural finish fish he was carving were being purchased as quickly as he carved them.

When the furniture company that Rick worked for moved their manufacturing operation out-of-state, he decided to carve full-time instead of holding another job.

Now his carvings keep him in his studio seven days a week and up to 16 hours a day. Although he spends some time carving loons and painted fish, Rick still has a dedication to the natural finish fish carvings for which he is known.

While fishing with Rick for the past 10 years, I have had the opportunity to share in his knowledge of fish and his imagination of life underwater. Rick has helped accelerate my carving career, and this book is sure to inspire many more people to become great fish carvers.

—Fred DacQuisto

ACKNOWLEDGMENTS

I must first express my appreciation to the many collectors who have gotten my carving career to where it is today. Without people collecting my work, I wouldn't be able to write this book and proceed with carving.

I am also very thankful to my friends and family for taking time to help me in my various undertakings. Most of all, I must thank fellow carver, friend, and fishing partner, Fred DacQuisto, of Racine, Wisconsin, for his constant support of all my endeavors.

Special thanks are in order for my good friend, Rob Maass from Rhinelander, Wisconsin, for always finding the specimens I need. Rob has helped me find not only the kind of fish I need, but also the right size.

Jon Bolton and Harvey Nyien from Racine, Wisconsin, deserve a thank you for a fine job on the photography. I would also like to thank my friend, John Maloney from Downers Grove, Illinois, for sharing his knowledge.

I greatly appreciate the help and assistance of Randy Feest of Woodcrafters Supply in Racine, Wisconsin. He has been a great source of information and supplies.

Last but certainly not least, I would like to thank my wife, Nancy, for all her assistance with the book, our gallery, and my career; and my two children, Tony and Marla, for putting up with my countless hours in the workshop.
Thanks.

Rick

INTRODUCTION

Fish carving can be a very relaxing hobby or a very stimulating and exciting art career. Whichever the case, by using the step-by-step instructions outlined in this book, fish carving is made easy. *Decorative Fish Carving* gives a very detailed look at the endeavor. The book not only gives explicit instructions, but also gives exact bit numbers and tool specifications. This will ensure that the beginning carver is using the proper woods, procedures, and tools for each step in the creation of a beautiful wood carving.

It is my belief that fish carving is the biggest up-and-coming form of realistic wood carving. In the future, it is certain that all decoy competitions will incorporate fish carving categories.

At present, natural wood fish carvings are a very minor part of the fish carving spectrum. As an art dealer who knows the demand for natural finish works, I have to believe specific categories will open for natural finish in competitions.

While fish carving is now in its infant stages, it is certain to grow and have a large impact on the art industry. I encourage all carvers to pay much attention to the artistic aspects of their works. Wildlife carving has been perfected to the point that future carving competition judges will select pieces that are most original and have the best overall composition. These artistic aspects are discussed briefly in chapter 7.

As the newest form of decorative wildlife carving, fish carving is growing rapidly, and the natural finish style of fish carving has the greatest potential for artistic originality and expression.

Getting Started

CHAPTER 1

Following are some of the basic tools you will need for basic fish carving. There are a variety of power tools available today. I personally like Dremel's variable speed Moto-Flex tool. I suggest that beginning carvers use this tool because it is inexpensive and does a fine job (FIG. 1-1).

Power tools

A band saw is the most frequently used tool other than the Moto-Tool by power carvers. If purchasing a band saw, I would advise getting a saw with a minimum of 6-inch cutting height (FIG. 1-2)

Another power tool often used in certain carving applications is the sander. There are small, less expensive sanders such as Dremel #730; the larger, more expensive models have much more power, but don't have the 1-inch belt which helps a great deal sanding and shaping small contours (FIGS. 1-3 and 1-4)

Chisels and knives

Although I personally rarely use knives and chisels, sometimes they are helpful in certain applications. A small set of sharp knives or X-Acto tools may be helpful, though not necessary (FIG. 1-5)

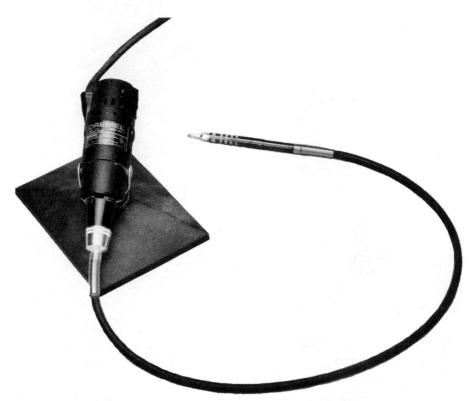

1-1   Dremel's variable speed Moto-Flex tool.

Rasps and rifflers

Rasps are very helpful in removing large amounts of wood quickly. Some rasps that may be quite useful are sure-form and straight rasps (FIG. 1-6)

Rifflers can also be helpful for small hard-to-get areas. Some small rifflers are pictured in FIG. 1-7.

Coping saw

The coping saw is a necessity when cutting small areas such as the tail because using a band saw to cut areas such as this is dangerous.

1-2   Band saw.   **1-3**   Dremel's disc belt sander.

Miscellaneous accessories

There are many miscellaneous accessories, most of which I have outlined below:

Wood burner   If attempting the painted fish in chapter 7, you will need a wood burner for detailing the face and burning in scales. I suggest a good wood burner because some less expensive burners get extremely hot after prolonged use. You should use a rheostat wood burner like the one pictured in FIG. 1-8. Smaller burner tips are desired for fish scaling.

Airbrush and compressor   Fish, unlike bird carvings, should be painted primarily with an airbrush to get a blended wet look. I use Badger airbrush #150-4, which is an excellent dual-action airbrush. A moisture trap should be installed between the compressor and the airbrush (FIG. 1-9)

1-4 Larger disc belt sander.

Paints For painted fish, you will need a complete set of paints. I suggest a complete set of Polytranspar airbrush paints and a complete set of Badger airbrush paints. See suppliers list. Refer to chapter 6 for color selection.

Oil Tung oil will be needed for natural finish fish. I use Formby's low-gloss tung oil, although Watco and Deft also make a good quality tung oil. Refer to chapter 4 for application techniques.

Other accessories

- Calipers or other similar measuring device
- Eye protection will be needed while using power tools
- Sandpaper—100- and 220-grit paper
- Dust mask

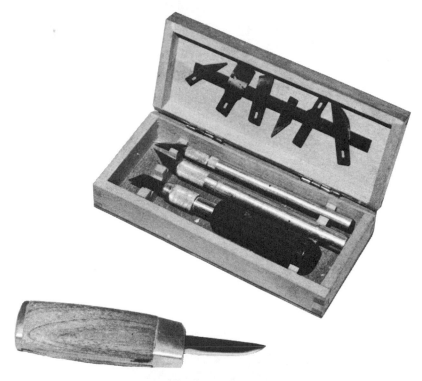

1-5   Exacto knives and handmade carving knife.

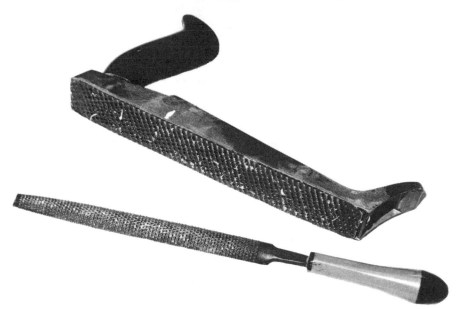

1-6   Sureform rasp and common wood rasp.

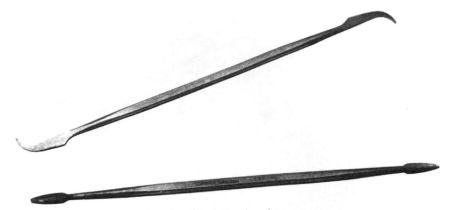

1-7   Small rifflers for hard-to-get areas.

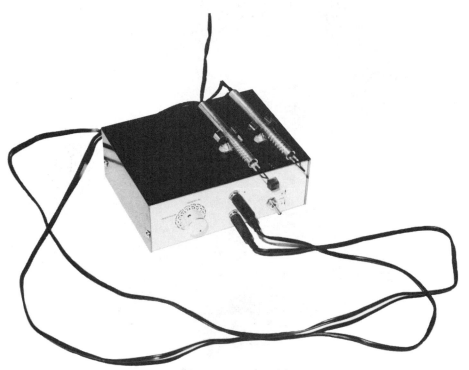

1-8   Rheostat type wood burner.

Moto-Tool bits used in this book

Dremel bit numbers 144, 116, 199, 408, 432, 411, 134, 190, 191, 105, 110, 189, 403, 922, 904, 974, 984, and 9912.

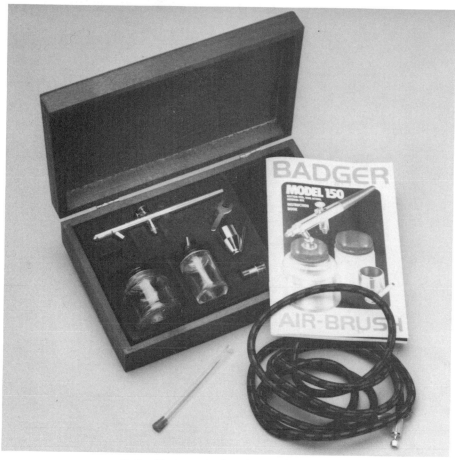

1-9 Badger dual action airbrush.

Selecting
Wood

CHAPTER 2

Although almost any wood can be used in carving, certain woods are preferred because of density and grain consistency. For natural finish carvings, woods with a smooth grain should be chosen.

Hardwood

Good carving hardwoods include cherry, butternut (hard to find), walnut, red elm, and rosewood (extremely hard). Although these woods can be very dense and hard, the final product will justify all the extra work.

I prefer and use cherry for the majority of my work.

Normally, eight-quarter hardwoods are the thickest I use. I choose to laminate any carvings wider than two inches because larger dimensioned blocks tend to check or crack over time.

Softwood

Today, three primary carving softwoods are used: basswood, jelutong, and tupelo. Each has advantages and disadvantages.

Basswood Basswood is very widely used in decoy carving. It is a soft, grainless wood with varying hardness. It's good for carvers that use knives and chisels, but isn't very good for power carving. Basswood fuzzes considerably when subject to power carving or sanding.

Jelutong Jelutong, an imported wood, is heavier than basswood and is good for power carving. Jelutong also has its disadvantages. It has latex pockets that may show up anywhere in the wood. These latex pockets are approximately 1/4-inch wide and 1/32-inch thick and may be any length. They are easily removed. I fill the holes with wood glue and wood slivers. Another disadvantage is that the wood grain has a very open pitted consistency to it. This wood doesn't detail as well as basswood or tupelo.

Tupelo Tupelo comes from the deep south. Carvers can obtain large blocks of this wood fairly easily. This wood is almost grainless and carves well with knives or power tools. This wood also details very well.

Tupelo does have its disadvantages. It is very inconsistent. One block may be soft and perfect for carving, and the next heavy and hard as a rock. Some pieces may be inconsistent from one side to the other. The best pieces will be the lighter weight blocks that are cut from the outer portion of the tree.

Tupelo carves easier when it is somewhat wet. As it dries, it becomes harder to carve. I wrap carvings in plastic when I'm not working on them to preserve moisture content. Although inconsistent, I prefer tupelo over other softwoods for painted carvings. Refer to suppliers list.

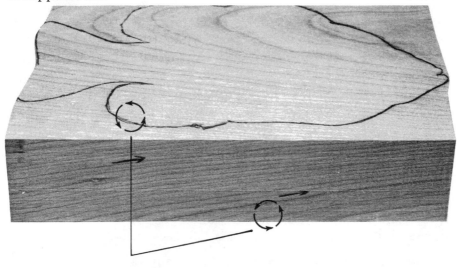

Bit rotation

2-1 Bit rotation should follow the direction of the grain.

When carving any wood, you should always be aware of grain direction, although this may be difficult while following contours of the fish. Carving with the grain will eliminate most chipping and fuzzing (FIG. 2-1). Note the bit direction in relation to grain lines on the wood.

Fish
Anatomy

CHAPTER 3

The next pages will show close-up photography of some fish and certain parts of fish, with brief description for your reference. Knowing anatomy is very important in all carving—whether fish, bird, or mammal.

Knowing anatomy

All fish carved for competition must be anatomically correct. Others which won't be judged will be much more impressive if anatomically correct.

- Figure 3-1 shows rainbow trout. Fin location.
- Figure 3-2 shows smallmouth bass. Head and body parts.
- Figure 3-3 shows smallmouth bass. Lower head and body parts.
- Figure 3-4 shows yellow perch. Lower body, discharge vent, etc.

Knowing fish movements

While knowing anatomy is very important, knowledge of fish action, fin movements, and attack positions of specific fish is also important. For example, pike, such as musky and northern, coil into an S-shape position before attack. A bass would attack from more of a

3-1   Rainbow trout fin location.

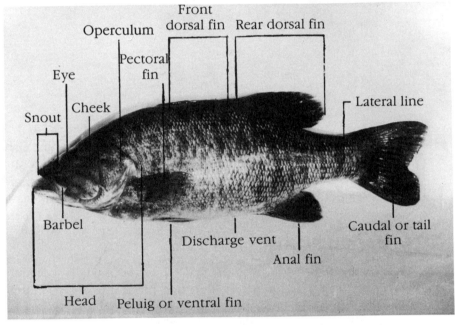

3-2   Smallmouth bass. Head and body parts.

horseshoe shape, while trout and salmon are normally cruising fish and usually don't bend much.

Figures 3-5 through 3-17 show some basic fin and body movements of crappie, sunfish, and bass.

Although this book contains numerous reference photos, nothing can compare with studying fish fresh out of the water. Every carver should develop his or her own reference library of photography. Now, whenever you want to go fishing, you have an excuse. You are going to do your reference work. You have to catch fish!

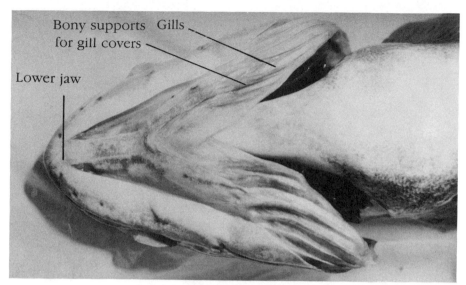

3-3   Smallmouth bass. Lower jaw.

3-4   Yellow perch. Lower body, discharge vent, etc.

3-5   Tail shape changes drastically when thrusted sideways.

3-6   Fins are all erect on the bass. Perch tail is in full motion.

3-7   Pectoral fins are usually in totally different positions from each other.

3-8   Notice the positions of the pectoral fin and half erect dorsal fin of this bass.

3-9 Notice the flow and turn of the anal and dorsal fins on this bass.

3-10 Notice the flowing fins on this black crappie and the position of the pectoral fin.

3-11 The dorsal fin on black crappies is rarely in the erect position.

3-12   This is a very good action pose for a wood carving with excellent fin position.

3-13   Girth shape and pectoral fin position on a crappie.

3-14   Notice the fin positions on these sunfish.

3-15 These sunfish fins are all fully erect.

3-16 Notice the girth shape
of this sunfish.

3-17 This sunfish has very exciting fin positioning.

Carving a Bluegill

CHAPTER 4

Bluegills are a very plentiful fish. They can be found in all 48 mainland states. Bluegills are spunky fish when hooked. They will flutter sideways, causing much resistance to an angler's line. Most anglers will catch bluegills between six to nine inches. Their girth may vary depending on time of year, feeding habits, and spawning periods. They can vary in size, shape, and color from lake to lake, or even within the same lake. There is no definite shape or color to any bluegill, although most bluegills are very similar. Bluegills' basic colors may range from pale green to purple, and color will be brighter if caught in cold water.

Bluegills have large flowing fins and when carved, are very aesthetically pleasing with or without paint. I have found that bluegills are the most well-known of all fish; therefore, the demand for bluegill carvings is high.

Roughing-out the carving

The first step is to select a piece of hardwood as discussed in chapter 2. For this carving, you will need a block of 8/4 hardwood (cherry in this case). This should be an approximately 9-×-6-inch block.

Begin by tracing the pattern onto the block of wood. First, trace the side view of the fish onto the block (FIG. 4-1). Proceed to cut just to

4-1   Trace side view of pattern on block and cut out with band saw.

the outside of your lines on the band saw. After the flat side cut has been made (FIG. 4-2), turn the fish block on end, sketching the top pattern onto the upper part of the block (FIG. 4-3). After you've sketched the top pattern onto the block, proceed to cut the top to bottom cuts into the fish (FIG. 4-4), then cut back of tail flat (FIG. 4-5).

4-2   Cut profile of fish with band saw.

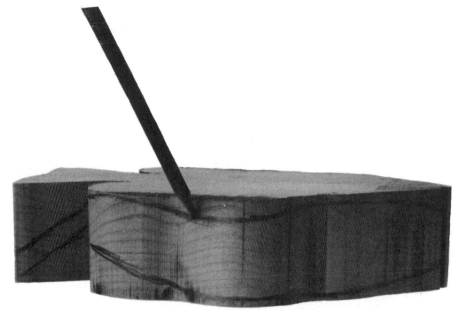

4-3 Sketch the top pattern onto the upper part of the fish.

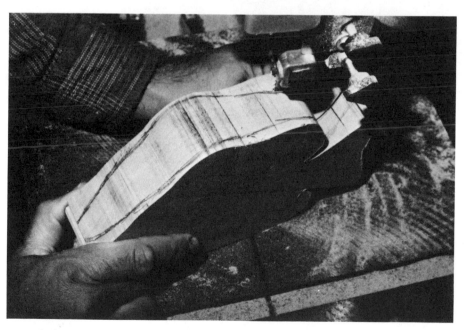

4-4 Proceed to cut the top to bottom cuts with the band saw.

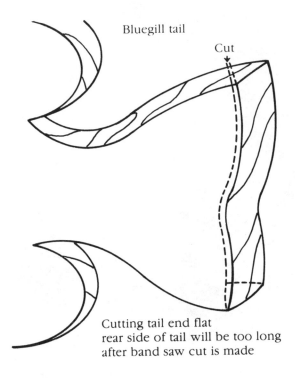

Bluegill tail

Cut

4-5   Cut back of tail flat.

Cutting tail end flat
rear side of tail will be too long
after band saw cut is made

Note: Pattern shows extra wood around anal, dorsal, and caudal fin areas in order to achieve the most action and movement possible in fin areas.

When carving natural finish, I feel it is important to portray as much action and flow as possible.

Reference marks should now be drawn onto the fish blank where the dorsal and anal fins join the body of the fish. Reference marks on the sides of the fish may be taken from the pattern (FIG. 4-6), and reference marks showing upper and lower views of the fins should be taken from the pattern.

For your first fish, you may want to keep the fins fairly simple. I suggest you leave a minimum of 1/4-inch of wood all along the fins. Allow plenty of wood for fin movement, especially on bluegills, because of their large flowing fins.

The cuts to remove this extra wood around the dorsal fins are made by putting your band saw at a 45-degree table angle and following the lines. Extend those cuts onto the forehead and face area to round off the top of the head. Be sure to leave enough wood for protruding eyes.

The cuts to remove the extra wood around the anal fin are extended onto the lower stomach sides (FIG. 4-7).

4-6   Draw reference line at base of anal and dorsal fins.

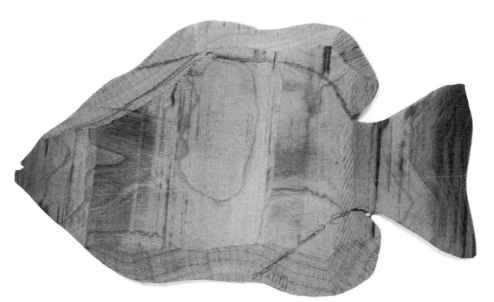

4-7   Extend angled band saw cuts onto forehead and belly.

Next, retrace the side reference marks where the body meets the dorsal and anal fins. Remove all excess wood on either side of the fins. When removing this wood, use a large cutter such as Dremel bit #134 or #144 or Cutsall bit (FIG. 4-8).

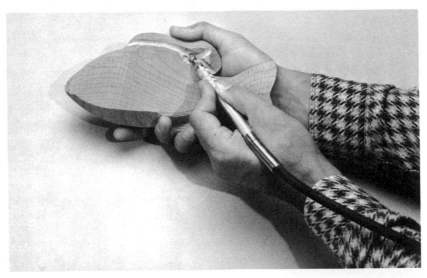

4-8   Remove excess wood with Dremel bit #144 on sides of anal and dorsal fins.

Refer to the pattern to obtain the proper girth shape. Measure the pattern from the nose to the area of the opercle and make this your first cut. Leave enough wood behind the opercle for the pectoral muscle. Use Dremel bit #116. When using this bit and other bits with square or angular edges, use extreme caution. These bits can cause a lot of damage.

If you don't have a band saw or the use of a band saw, fish blanks can be ordered from:

BEYER GALLERIES
1115 N. Main Street
Racine, Wisconsin 53402

Both body and fin blanks will be at this stage of completion (FIGS. 4-9 and 4-10).

When corresponding for pricing, specify hardwood, softwood, type of fish, and size.

Next, put the fish into the vise and sketch the desired curve onto the end of the tail. In this case, it is an S-shaped curve. The markings on this caudal fin are approximately 1/8-inch or 3/16-inch wide. The wood is removed outside of the marks with a coping saw (FIG. 4-11). The caudal fin will be left alone until the rest of the fish is roughed-in. This is to prevent accidental breakage of the caudal fin.

Band saw cuts

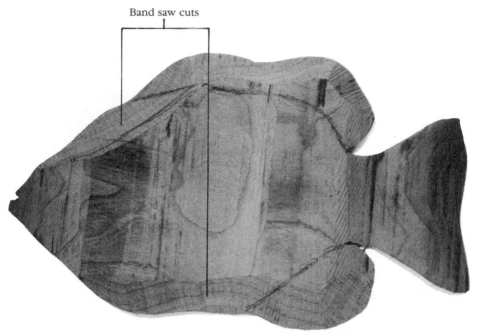

4-9   Body blank will be at this stage of completion.

4-10   Fins for fish blanks will be in this stage of completion.

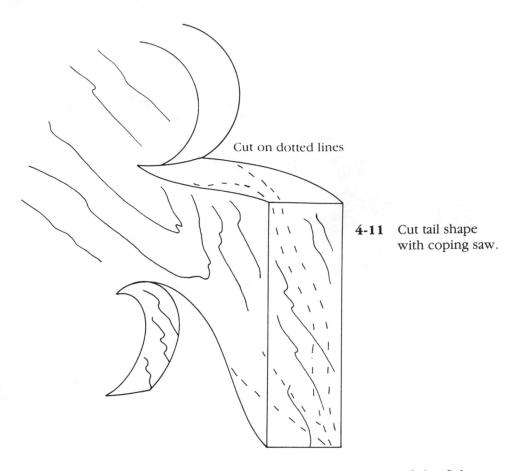

Cut on dotted lines

4-11 Cut tail shape with coping saw.

Proceed to draw in the line that separates the body of the fish from the caudal fin (FIGS. 4-12 and 4-13). This line is a double arch-shaped line. Remove the extra wood on the tail side of that line. Next, cut away wood in front of the line, gradually tapering the body into the tail. Also, taper the wood from the edge of the caudal fin to the front of the fin. Do not make the caudal fin too thin at this time.

Starting the details

After roughing-in the caudal fin, remove all carving marks and indentations with a Dremel drum sander #408. When smooth, draw in the operculum and other face markings (FIG. 4-14).

At this point, symmetry becomes very important. Symmetry should be checked constantly as you proceed from this stage.

Using the Dremel bit #199, undercut the gill covers starting even with or just above the pectoral fin muscle. Cut down to the lower jaw

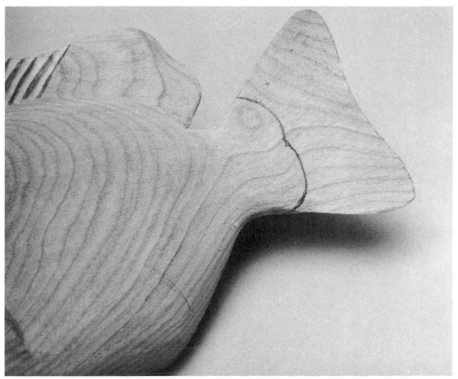

4-12   Draw in line separating body of fish from caudal fin.

4-13   View of actual peduncle.

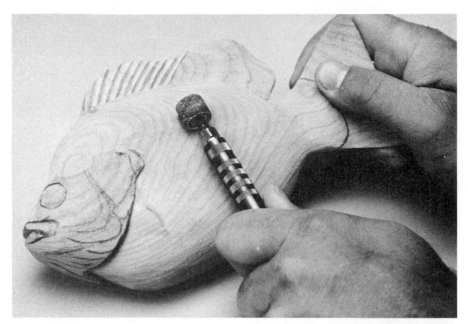

4-14 Rough sand with Dremel drum sander #408 and draw in face markings.

(FIG. 4-15). Cut at the greatest angle possible to portray the gill covers folding under the fish.

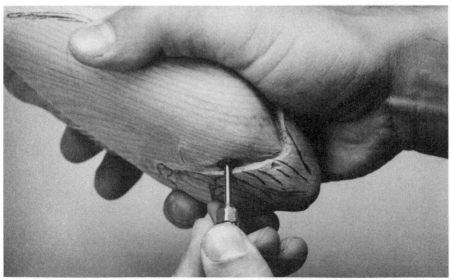

4-15 Undercut gill covers with Dremel bit #199.

Draw in the eye, and check symmetry. Cut around the eyes with Dremel bit #190. The eye may be shaped slightly downward or straight up and down (FIGS. 4-16 and 4-17). Continue to use slower speeds on most bits when carving hardwoods.

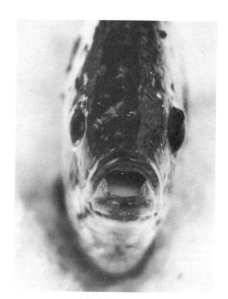

4-16 Front view of live bluegill eye positions.

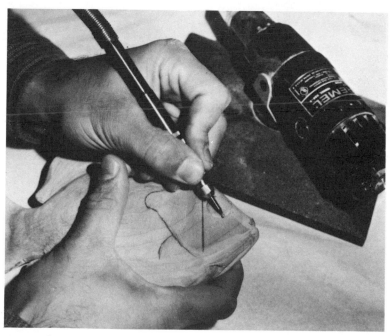

4-17 Cut around the eyes with Dremel bit #190.

Many times on larger and fatter fish, rib cage and stomach protrusions must be drawn in at this time. Many fish have double girths or indentations between muscle and other body parts. Use Dremel bit #144 and finish with Dremel drum sander #408 (FIG. 4-18).

4-18   Larger fish may have indentations above belly. Also note dorsal or anal fins may be inlaid.

If mistakes are made on dorsal or anal fins, they may also be inlaid, although not preferred (FIG. 4-19).

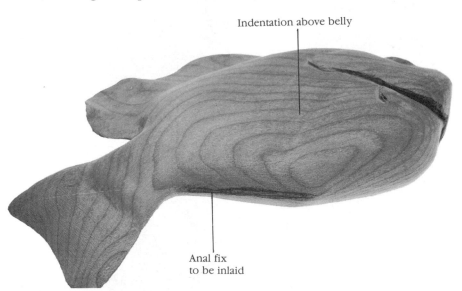

Indentation above belly

Anal fix
to be inlaid

4-19   If mistakes are made on dorsal or anal fins, they may also be inlaid although not preferred.

Most of the face, including the eyes, operculum, lips, etc., are initially cut with a Dremel carbide cutter #9912. On hardwood, natural finish fish, some facial structure may have to be exaggerated because of the lack of paint or color to bring out facial features. Accuracy is important, although some stylistic exaggeration may increase the impact of the piece (FIGS. 4-20 and 4-21).

Carve in the bony shafts on the underside of gill covers. Use three shafts on either side. Check chapter 3 for reference photo.

4-20 Actual bluegill face features.

4-21 Face markings are roughed-in with Dremel bit #9912.

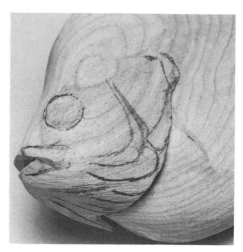

After the rib cage indentation and the gill covers and other head parts are roughed-in, the entire fish may be sanded to a smooth finish. The body, face, and fins should be sanded somewhat smooth. Start with a Dremel drum sander #408, then a drum sander #432 and finish with coarse discs.

Carving the fins

All fins on the main body (caudal, dorsal, and anal) should now be sanded to sharp edge (FIG. 4-22). Figure 4-23 shows fin location.

4-22   Sand fin edges with Dremel drum sander #408.

4-23   Fin location on male and female bluegill.

Proceed to draw the rays on the fins. Check the reference on the number of fin rays on each fin.

Anal fin   Three spines with 11 rays following. Total 14. (Figures 4-24 and 4-25.)

Front dorsal fin   10 spines (FIG. 4-26).

4-24   Anal fin of bluegill.

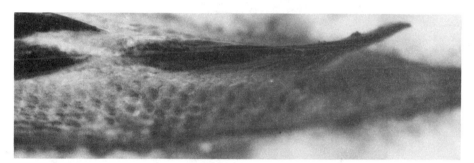

4-25   Bottom view of bluegill anal fin.

4-26   Front dorsal fin of bluegill.

Rear dorsal fin   12 rays that split $1/4$-inch from the body. Spines on the dorsal fins are stacked side-by-side when the fin lays down.

Caudal fin   Three short, spiny rays: top—eight; bottom—nine. The short top and bottom rays don't split (FIG. 4-27).

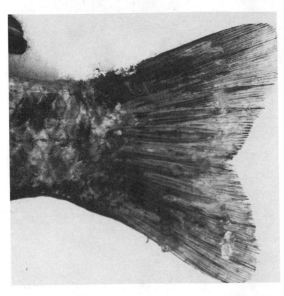

4-27   Caudal fin of bluegill. Notice ragged end.

Pectoral fins   Three rays: top—short, about $1/2$-inch to $3/4$-inch, bottom—short, about $1/4$-inch to $1/2$-inch (FIGS. 4-28 and 4-29).

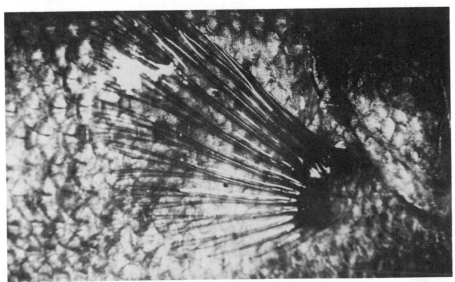

4-28   Pectoral fin of bluegill.

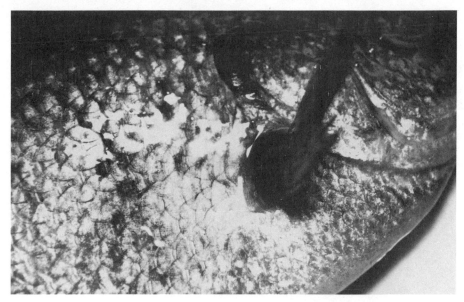

4-29 Pectoral fin extended. Muscle is visible.

Ventral fins One front spine with five fin rays following (FIG. 30).

The ventral and pectoral fins can be cut from the scrap wood cut from the main fish block. These fins should be cut so that fin rays run in the same direction as the wood grain. Allow approximately 1/4-inch to 3/8-inch width so that the fins can show a lot of flow and movement (FIG. 4-31). Proceed to cut the fins in the same manner as the anal and rear dorsal fins mentioned below (FIG. 4-32).

4-30 Erect ventral fin on bluegill.

4-31 Cut ventral and pectoral fins from scrap.

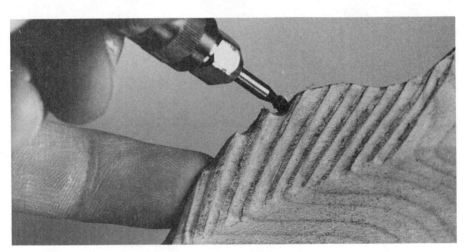

4-32 Cut between spines and front dorsal fin with round cutter.

After drawing in the fins, cut out the sections between the spines on the front dorsal fin using a coping saw or cutter #191. I suggest that you use a cutter and proceed with caution so you don't break the spines on the fins (FIG. 4-33). Proceed with a smaller cutter, Dremel #110, cutting 3/4 of the way up the fin. Divide all the fin rays into split fin rays and repeat the procedure until the fins are adequately split (FIGS. 4-34 through 4-37). Some fins are completely split to the body and some only partially. Finish defuzzing and sanding all the fins using the Dremel coarse disc #411 and bristle brush #403.

4-33   Dorsal, anal, and caudal fins with initial cuts.

4-34   Pectoral fins with initial cuts.

4-35   Pectoral fin with rays divided one time.

4-36   Fully divided rays on pectoral fin. Note splits at end of fin.

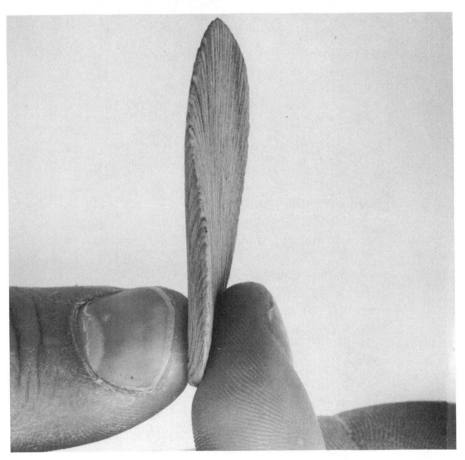

4-37   Always portray motion by curving fins.

Finishing touches

At this point, the discharge vent may be carved in with Dremel bit #
189. The vent is a shallow crater-shaped opening (FIG. 4-38).

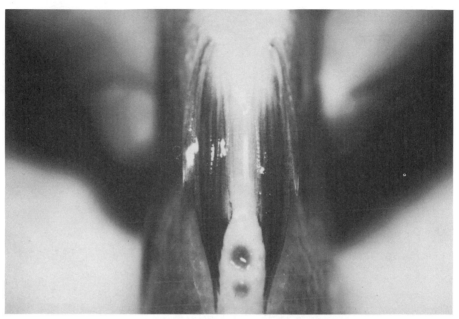

4-38   Ventral fin location in relation to discharge vent.

Then, drill in the nostrils with Dremel bit #105. The nostrils are
located approximately $3/16$-inch in front of the eyes and are double
nostrils on each side (FIG. 4-39).

While holding the ventral and pectoral fins against the fish body,
draw the outline of the base of the fin onto the body, one at a time.
Using Dremel cutters #190 and #105, carve a hole at the desired fin
angle. Refer to chapter 3 for reference on fin angles. Carve the hole
slightly smaller than the outline and repeatedly fit the fin into the
hole. These holes must be extremely accurate on natural finish fish.

After the holes are carved and the fins fit accurately, make muscle
markings around fin holes. The pelvic muscles are usually elongated
lumps (FIG. 4-40).

All finish-sanding may be done to the entire fish at this time. I
begin with 100-grit sandpaper, then use 220-grit sandpaper to complete sanding. Check trout chapter for tips on sanding fins.

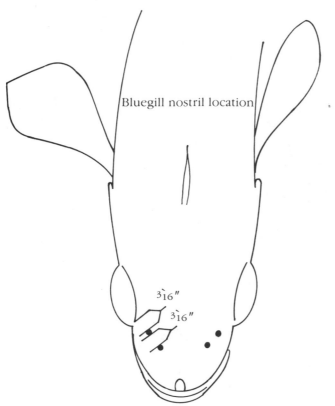

Bluegill nostril location

$3\tfrac{\grave{}}{16}''$

$3\tfrac{\grave{}}{16}''$

4-39   Nostril location.

4-40   Carve holes for ventral and pectoral fins.

After finish-sanding is complete, glue fins into place using Elmer's wood glue. When fins are installed, glue may seep out sides of the fins. This excess glue must be completely removed, or the tung oil finish will not absorb in these areas.

After the glue has dried, preferably overnight, apply one coat of tung oil. This may be done in different ways.

1. Apply Formby's low or high gloss tung oil with small artist's brush and wipe off with lint-free tissue or rag. Rub lightly with steel wool after completely dry. Remove all dust. Then apply a second coat, wiping off all excess tung oil (FIG. 4-41).

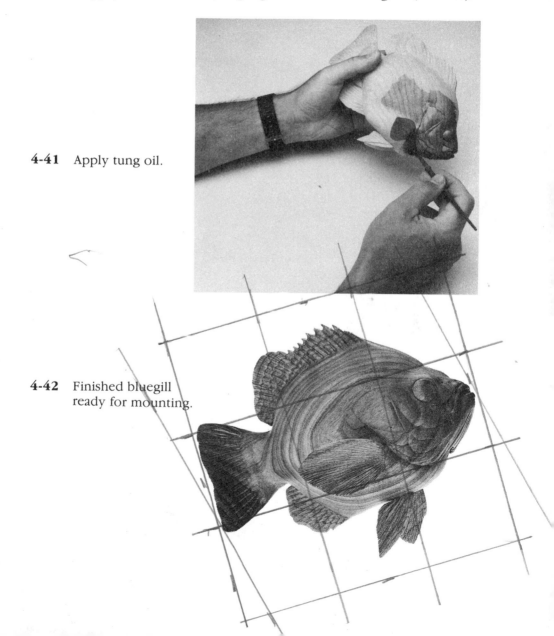

4-41 Apply tung oil.

4-42 Finished bluegill ready for mounting.

2. Apply a Watco tung oil (which has no varnish). Liberally rub into finish using steel wool. Wipe completely off. Let first coat dry completely, then rub in second coat, wiping off all excess tung oil. A third and fourth coat may be desired.

Your bluegill is now complete (FIG. 4-42), with the exception of the mount. Mounting fish into scenes or onto basic mounts is discussed in chapter 7.

Largemouth Bass—''Frog Legs.''

Basic Bluegill wall hanging.

Largemouth Bass—"Final Battle."

Walleyes—"Feeding Frenzy."

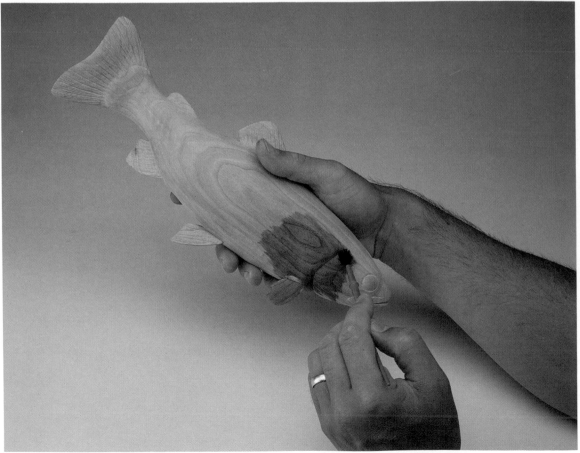

ABOVE: Tropical fish aquarium—"Tropical Delight."

TOP LEFT: Completed trout ready for mounting.

BOTTOM LEFT: Applying tung oil to trout.

Applying light bass green to upper 2/3 of fish.

Stripes applied by spraying back 1/2 of scales.

Sienna color between fin rays.

Equal balance and flow in all directions.

The ultimate fish carving—"Ambush."

Carving
trout

CHAPTER 5

When talking trout, the first vision that comes to mind is that of the fly rod whipping as the angler skillfully places his dry fly above the awaiting trout in his favorite secluded stream. This may possibly be the ultimate in leisure sportfishing.

Whether stream fishing with fly rods, trolling with downriggers, or ice fishing frozen lakes, trout fishing always proves exciting when you're lucky enough to bag an elusive trout or two.

There are a variety of trout species, including rainbow, brown, brook, cutthroat and lake trout.

In this chapter, we will concentrate on the rainbow trout. Rainbows are named for the colored bands on the sides of the fish. They may range in size anywhere from fingerlings to 30-some pounds.

Rainbows fresh out of water, especially smaller ones, have many beautiful iridescent colors. They tend to lose these colors quickly when out of water.

Trout are very smooth, sleek-looking fish. They are aesthetically pleasing when carved in natural hardwood or when painted.

Trout are possibly the easiest fish to carve in natural hardwood because when the color is removed, they are a very simple shaped fish with very little fin structure. The rainbow trout would be an excellent fish for the beginning carver to start on. When carving trout to be painted, refer to chapter 6 for different carving techniques on softwoods.

Roughing-out the carving

The first step is to select a piece of hardwood as discussed in chapter 2. For this carving, you will need a block of 8/4 hardwood (cherry in this case). This should be an approximately 16-×-5-inch block.

Begin by tracing the pattern onto the block of wood (FIG. 5-1). First, trace the side view of the fish onto the block. Proceed to cut just to the outside of your lines on the band saw (FIG. 5-2). After the flat side cut has been made, turn the fish block on end, sketching the top pattern onto the upper part of the block (FIG. 5-3). After you've sketched the top pattern onto the block, proceed to cut the top to bottom cuts into the fish, then cut back of tail flat (FIG. 5-4). Because trout fins are small, most of the movement will be in the tail area.

Reference marks should now be drawn onto the fish blank for width on dorsal, adipose, and anal fins of the fish. Reference marks

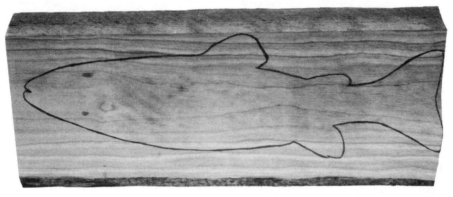

5-1   Trace the side view onto block.

5-2   Cut out with the band saw.

5-3 Sketch the top pattern onto upper part of block and cut out with the band saw.

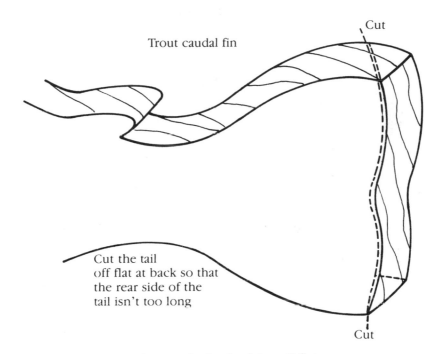

Trout caudal fin

Cut

Cut the tail
off flat at back so that
the rear side of the
tail isn't too long

Cut

5-4 Cut the back of the tail flat.

on the sides of the fish may be taken from the pattern; reference marks showing upper and lower views of the fins should be taken from the reference photos of the live fish. I suggest you leave a minimum of 1/4-inch of wood all along the fins.

The cuts to remove this extra wood around the dorsal fins are made by putting your band saw at a 45-degree table angle and following the lines. Extend those cuts onto the forehead and face area to round-off the top of the head. Be sure to leave enough wood for the protruding eyes, especially on trout, which have large, protruding eyes (FIG. 5-5).

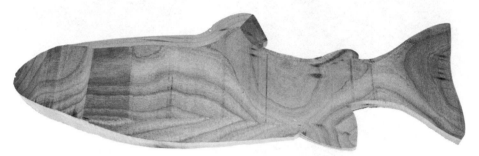

5-5   Cut extra wood on corners of fish with band saw.

The cuts to remove the extra wood around the anal fin are extended onto the lower stomach sides.

Next, shape the girth of the fish, using the pattern for reference, with a rasp (FIG. 5-6). Sand off the rough-rasped surface with a Dremel drum sander #408.

5-6   Roughed-in trout after rasping.

Next, retrace the side reference marks where the body meets the dorsal, adipose, and anal fins. Remove all excess wood on either side of these fins. When removing this wood, use a large cutter such as a Dremel bit #134 or #144 or Cutsall bit (FIG. 5-7). After the wood is removed on the anal, adipose, and dorsal fins to approximately 1/8-inch thickness, sand the body of fish near the anal, adipose, and dorsal fins with drum sander #408.

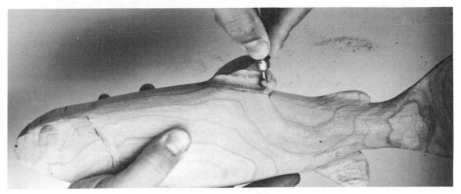

5-7 Remove excess wood from both sides of fins.

Next, put fish into vise and sketch desired curve onto the end of the tail. In this case, it is an S-shaped curve. If a different tail action is desired,, refer to the chapter on anatomy for reference and ideas. The markings on this caudal fin are approximately $1/8$-inch to $3/16$-inch wide. The wood is removed outside of the two parallel S-shaped lines with a coping saw, leaving thicker wood toward the body side of the caudal fin (FIG. 5-8). Given the chance of breakage, the caudal fin will be left alone until the rest of the fish is roughed-in.

5-8 Draw marking on end of tail. Put the fish in a vise and cut outside of parallel lines with coping saw.

Proceed to draw in the line that separates the body of the fish from the caudal fin, using reference on actual fish (FIG. 5-9). Then remove extra wood in the tail side of that line.

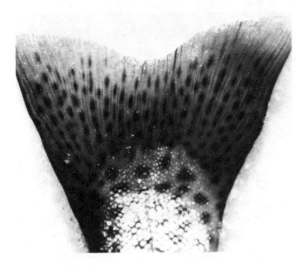

5-9 View of how caudal fin attaches to the peduncle.

Next, cut away wood in front of the line, gradually tapering the peduncle into the tail. Also, taper the wood from the edge of the caudal fin to the front of the fin. Do not make the caudal fin too thin at this time.

Starting the details

After roughing-in the caudal fin, remove all carving marks and indentations with drum sander #408 (FIG. 5-10). When smooth, draw in operculum and face markings (FIGS. 5-11 through 5-13).

Next, check symmetry. Measure pattern from nose to rear of operculum and make this your first cut. Leave enough wood behind operculum for the pectoral muscle. Using Dremel bit #199, undercut gill covers starting just above pectoral fin muscle and cut down under gill covers (FIG. 5-14). Cut at the greatest angle possible to portray gill covers folding under fish, which on trout are very fleshy (FIG. 5-15).

After the markings are drawn on the face and operculum, draw in the eyes. Check symmetry. Cut around eyes with Dremel bit #190 (FIG. 5-16). Eyes may be shaped slightly downward or straight up and down. Continue to use slower speeds on most bits when carving hardwoods.

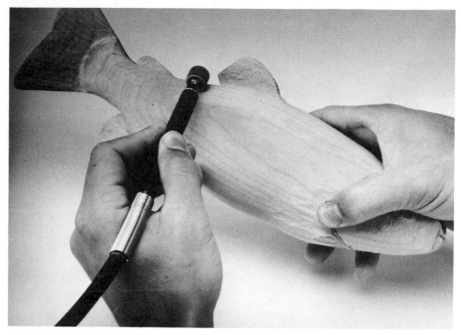

5-10 Remove all carving marks with Dremel drum sander #408.

5-11 Underside of jaw on rainbow trout.

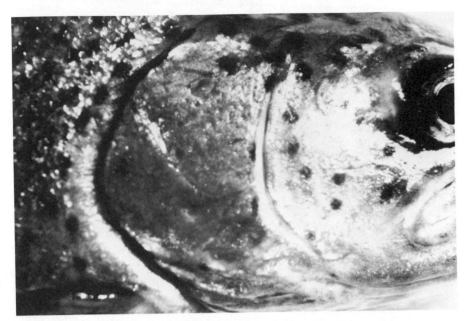

5-12   Operculum on rainbow trout.

5-13   Front of head and nostril position on rainbow trout.

5-14 Undercut gill covers with Dremel bit #199.

5-15 Underside of jaw on rainbow trout.

On larger, fatter fish, many times rib cage and stomach protrusions must be drawn in at this time. Trout have double girths and indentations between muscles and other body parts. Use Dremel bit #144 and finish with Dremel drum sander #408. (Figures 5-17 and 5-18.)

Most of the face, including eyes, lips, etc., are initially cut with carbide cutter #9912. Remove wood above eyes using the crisscross lines as guidelines. Remove with Dremel bit #144 (FIG. 5-19).

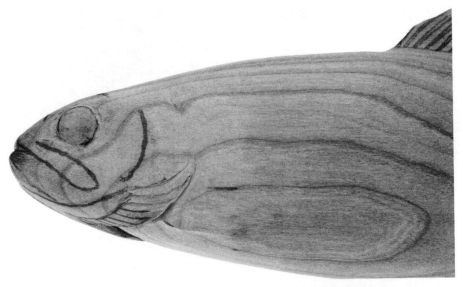

5-16   Cut around eyes with Dremel bit #190.

5-17   Draw in muscle indentations.

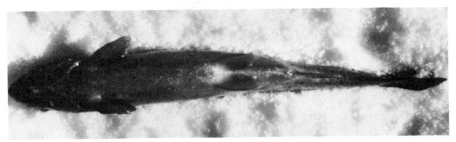

5-18   Photo of actual contour of trout's lower body.

5-19 Use crisscross line on forehead for reference.

After rib cage indentations, operculum, and facial parts are roughed-in, the entire fish may be sanded to a smooth finish. The body, face, and fins should be sanded somewhat smooth. Start with Dremel drum sander #408, drum sander #432, and finish with coarse disc #411.

Carving the fins

All fins on main body, caudal, dorsal, and anal fins should now be sanded to a sharp edge. Use Dremel drum sanders #408 and #432.

Proceed to draw in the fin rays onto the fins. Check reference on the number of fin rays on each fin and refer to FIG. 3-1 for fin location.

Caudal fin Three outer spines, top and bottom (these are hard to count because they are fleshy) and 16 fin rays in between. All rays are split completely to tail muscle (FIG. 5-9).

Anal fin One short spine followed by 11 fin rays, all splitting approximately 1/4-inch from body (FIG. 5-20).

Dorsal fin One front spine and 11 rays following. These 11 rays split almost immediately from the body. All fin rays are fleshier on trout than on game fish (FIG. 5-21).

5-20   Anal fin on rainbow trout.

5-21   Dorsal fin on rainbow trout.

Pelvic or ventral fins   These 10 rays split almost at the point where they meet the body (FIGS. 5-22 and 5-23). There is also a scaled extremity that protrudes from the base of the pelvic fin and is approximately 5/8-inch in length.

5-22   Ventral fins on rainbow trout.

5-23   Close-up of ventral fins.

Pectoral fins   Approximately 13 fin rays that split almost at the point where they meet the body. Spines on the dorsal fin are stacked side-by-side when the fin lays down. The pectoral fins have 13 rays. The bottom ray is short, about 1/4-inch to 1/2-inch. The top ray is short, about 1/2-inch to 3/4-inch. The pelvic fins have a front spine and five fin rays following the front spine (FIGS. 5-24 and 5-25).

Adipose fin   Fleshy, limp, no rays.

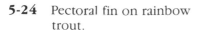

5-24   Pectoral fin on rainbow trout.

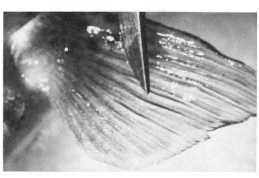

5-25   Pectoral fin location.

Cut between the rays with Dremel bit #189, #190, or #191. Proceed with smaller cutter #109. Divide all fin rays into split fin rays and repeat procedure until fins are adequately split (FIG. 5-26). Some fins are split completely to body, some only partially.

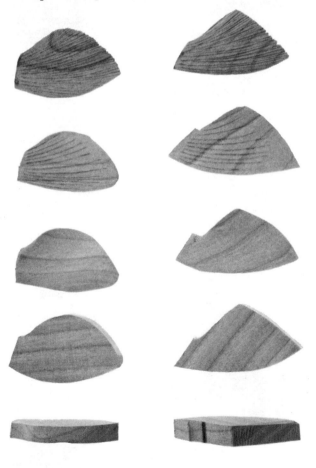

5-26   Cut between fin rays on ventral and pectoral fins. Divide fin rays until adequately divided.

Finish defuzzing and sanding all fins using coarse disc #411 and bristle brush #403. Hold sanding discs perpendicular to the fins when sanding. First, lightly sand the fin from one side, then turn the fin and lightly sand the opposite side of the fin ray (FIGS. 5-27 through 5-29).

5-27 Sand grooves of fins with coarse sanding disc edge.

5-28 Sand opposite sides of grooves with coarse sanding disc edge.

5-29 Defuzz fins with bristle brush #403.

Finishing touches

The discharge vent—a shallow crater-shaped opening—may be carved in at this point. It is located immediately in front of the anal fin (FIG. 5-30). Also, drill in nostrils at this time with Dremel bit #105. There are two nostrils on each side of the head, the first located approximately 1/4-inch from the front of the eye and the other located approximately 1/4-inch from the first, inward and toward the tip of the head (FIGS. 5-13 and 5-31).

5-30   Location of discharge vent on rainbow trout.

5-31   Draw outline of base of ventral and pectoral fins onto fish and carve at desired fin angle.

While holding the pelvic or pectoral fins against the fish body, one at a time, draw the outline of the base of the fin onto the body.

Using cutters #190 and #105, carve a hole at the desired fin angle. Carve the hole slightly smaller than the outline and repeatedly fit fin to hole. These holes must be extremely accurate on a natural finish fish (FIG. 5-32).

After the holes are carved and the fins fit accurately, make muscle markings around fin holes. The pelvic muscles are usually elongated lumps (FIGS. 5-18 and 5-25).

All finish-sanding may be done to entire fish at this time. I begin with 100-grit sandpaper, then sand with 220 grit.

5-32 Repeatedly fit fins into holes.

Next, glue the fins into place using wood glue. When fins are installed, glue may seep out sides of fins. This excess glue must be completely removed. If glue is not removed, the tung oil finish will not absorb in these areas.

After the glue has dried, preferably overnight, apply one coat of tung oil. This may be done two different ways:

1. Apply Formby's low or high gloss tung oil with small artist brush and wipe off with lint-free tissue or rag. Rub lightly with steel wool after completely dry. Remove all dust. Then apply a second coat, wiping off all excess tung oil.

2. Apply a Watco tung oil (which is no varnish) liberally. Rub it into the finish using steel wool. Wipe it completely off. Let the first coat dry completely, then rub in a second coat, wiping off all excess tung oil. A third and fourth coat may be desired.

Your trout is now complete, with the exception of the mount. Mounting fish into scenes or onto basic mounts is discussed in chapter 7.

Carving

Painted

Perch

CHAPTER 6

When I think of fishing with my family as a youngster, I remember how exciting it was to catch a stringer full of perch, using a simple rod and reel, bobber, hook, and a piece of a worm. Since it was a very plentiful fish, it seemed you could catch perch anytime, anywhere. In this chapter, I'll discuss creating a school of fish just prior to the catch and show you how to produce life underwater.

Carving softwood

The beginning procedures are essentially the same for carving oiled hardwood fish and painted softwood fish.

For the perch carvings, I am using tupelo in a minimum of 2-×-4-×-10-inch blocks.

Follow the same procedures as in chapters 4 and 5 to draw the pattern onto the block and cut profile and top-to-bottom cuts into the block. The 45-degree angle cuts to shape the perch may also be cut in. Note different tail shapes in FIGS. 6-1 through 6-4.

From this point, the softwood carving becomes much easier than a hardwood carving. You will notice how much easier it is to remove excess wood from the body of the perch.

Continue to follow the carving instructions in chapters 4 and 5 until you reach the part on carving in face detail. To get sharp details on the face and gill plates, carve in basic shape and cuts with Dremel

6-1   Live perch tail position #1.

6-2   Live perch tail position #2.

6-3 Live perch tail position #3.

6-4 Perch position #4.

aluminum oxide wheel points #904 and #984, then hand-sand to the proper shape with 100-grit sandpaper. After viewing FIG. 6-5 on face detail, proceed to burn in the sharp details onto the face using the side of your wood burner tip. When turning tupelo, use low heat settings (FIG. 6-6).

6-5   Face detail of perch.

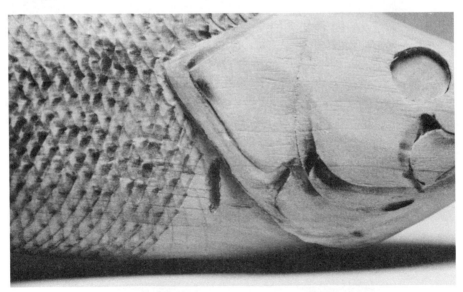

6-6   Use wood burner for face detail.

The entire fish should be sanded using 100-grit sandpaper followed by 220-grit paper. You will notice the casc in which these softwoods may be shaped. If using basswood, fuzzing may occur. To solve this problem, change the carving or sanding directions. Carve and sand "with" the grain.

When carving the fins, you may prefer using Dremel aluminum oxide wheel points #974 and #922 and reworking the bit to the right shape for different fins. This is done by putting the aluminum oxide wheel point into your moto tool, then taking a sharpening stone or other bit, molding the bit in the tool as it rotates (FIG. 6-7). *Note*: Although I use this procedure, it may not be recommended by the manufacturer. If you mold and rework your abrasive bits, proceed with extreme caution. (Do not try this with any high speed cutters!)

The tips of fins may also be wood burned to prevent fuzzing and to get sharp fin detail (FIG. 6-8).

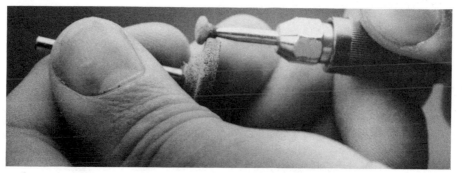

6-7 Use sharpening stone or other bit to shape bits to desired shape.

6-8 Tips of fins may be wood burned.

If you choose not to wood burn the tips of the fins, they may be carved with Dremel diamond wheel point #7120. This bit is used when dividing all of the fin rays on softwood carvings (FIG. 6-9). I prefer this method.

When carving the fins on the perch, note FIGS. 6-10 through 6-14.

Front dorsal fin   Has 12 rays (FIG. 6-10).

Rear dorsal fin   Has 14 rays, with the front two being spines and the back 12 dividing approximately $1/3$ of the way from the body (FIG. 6-11).

6-9   Alternate method using diamond wheel point #7120 (I prefer this method).

6-10   Front dorsal fin of perch.

6-11   Rear dorsal fin of perch.

Anal fin   Has nine rays, the front two being spines and the back seven dividing almost immediately from the body (FIG. 6-12).

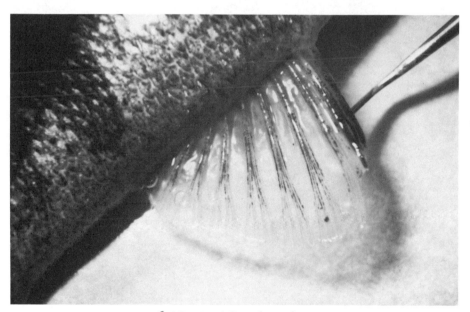

6-12   Anal fin of perch.

Ventral fins   Have six rays, the first being a spine and the back five dividing at the body (FIGS. 6-13 and 6-14).

Pectoral fins   Have approximately 11 rays, all dividing (FIG. 6-15).

Caudal fin   Has 18 rays, plus two or three short rays on top and bottom (FIG. 6-16).

6-13   Ventral fin of perch.

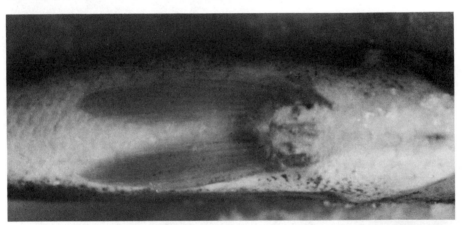

6-14   Positioning of ventral fins on perch.

6-15   Pectoral fin of perch.

6-16   Caudal fin of perch.

When cutting openings in the body of the perch for the fins, I usually cut the hole slightly small and carefully push the fin into the opening (FIG. 6-17). The softwood will usually expand slightly to accommodate the fin. Do not glue the pectoral and ventral fins in until you've completed the paint procedure.

6-17   Carefully push the fin into the opening.

The eyes must be cut out to accommodate the glass eyes (FIG. 6-6). For a 10-inch perch, I use 10mm Van Dyke general purpose fish eyes. (See suppliers list.) When cutting the eye hole, cut deep enough to move eyes into perfect symmetry. After cutting the eye holes, test eyes in sockets. If needed, build up with wood filler. Fill around eye with wood filler or epoxy putty. When epoxy putty or wood fillers are wet, they will have diverse effects on painted eyes.

To save yourself time removing paint, mask off the eyes with masking tape or rubber masking material. The edges may be blended later.

Carving the scales

To apply scales, start by drawing in the lateral line of the perch. Draw in diagonal lines from the middle of the back up to the lateral line. The lines should be approximately 1/8-inch apart and slightly closer together toward the tail and head (FIG. 6-18). Count rows of scales on actual fish for reference. Perch have approximately 75 rows of scales.

6-18   Draw in lateral line and then draw in diagonal lines to lateral line.

Using a small burner tip turned to its side, burn in the lower back side of the scales (FIG. 6-19). Next burn in the top back side of the next row of scales (FIG. 6-20). Figure 6-21 shows the finished scales.

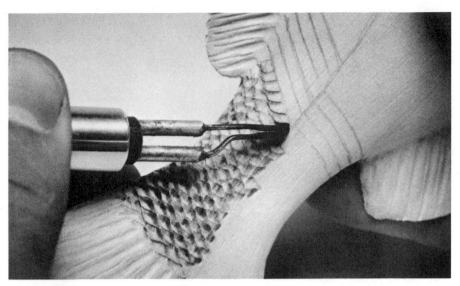

6-19 Burn lower backside of scales.

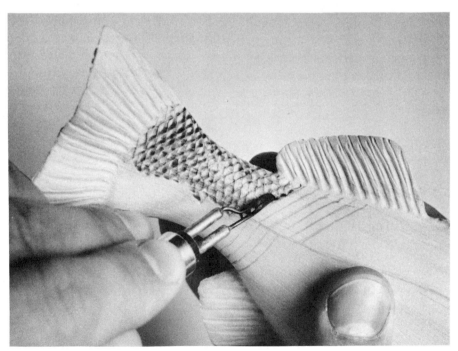

6-20 Burn in the top backside of the next row of scales.

6-21   Close-up of finished scales.

Notice the lines under the lateral line sometimes change direction from the lines above the lateral line, making the lateral line stand out. Finish scaling entire fish, starting from the tail and proceed forward. Notice that scales don't go completely onto the face (FIGS. 6-22 through 6-24). At this point, if the eyes haven't been installed, they should be glued in. Fill in around eyes with epoxy putty. Leave no gaps between glass eyes and eye sockets. The fish is now ready for paint.

Painting the fish

Although the Badger #150 is a very good airbrush, the artist must learn how to use and care for it to ensure good results. If you haven't used an airbrush before, you should spend a few hours with the airbrush before spraying your fish. A few basic rules to follow when airbrushing are:

1. Keep your airbrush clean at all times.
2. Keep the airbrush tip wet when you stop spraying so that paint doesn't dry on the tip.
3. Use an in-line moisture trap so your air is dry when it mixes with the paint.
4. Stir and shake your paint thoroughly and filter out all foreign particles in the paint.
5. Use the right head and needle for each particular job.

6-22 Progress photo of scaling procedure.

6-23 Notice scales don't go all the way onto the face.

6-24 Finished scaled fish ready for eyes. Front view.

The first step is to spray the fish with good quality wood primer. When spraying the primer, don't fill in the scale marks. Usually two thin coats of primer are desirable. A thin water base paint without primer will raise the grain in the wood. This can ruin the carving.

The perch in this chapter were primed with a beige automobile primer that can be used on wood. Polytranspar also carries a wood sealer. Good quality clear spray lacquer may also be used.

Because I need a wide color selection of paints for all fish species, I keep a supply of paints by different suppliers. There are two basic airbrush paints that I use:

1. Badger Opaque—Available at art and craft stores.
2. Polytranspar—Check supplies list.

Although I use both Badger and Polytranspar airbrush paints, to simplify the painting process, I will give a paint schedule using only Polytranspar paints on the perch. Colors needed for perch:

- Superhide white #WA10
- Yellow ochre #WA141
- Light bass green #WA60
- Gold transparent toner #WA360
- Yellow gold pearl #WA425
- Gill red (cadmium) #WA160
- Flesh #WA165

- Bright orange #WA90
- Medium bass green #WA61
- Sienna #WA200
- Wet look gloss #WA240

Besides the colors needed for perch, I suggest you add the following colors to your selection. Hopefully, by having extra colors, you will begin experimenting with these colors and develop your own paint schedules. I highly recommend both when carving and painting that you, as an artist, begin to develop your own style and procedures. Some extra colors that may be useful on other fish include:

- Satin white pearl essence #WA401
- Silver pearl essence #WA402
- Softest gold look pearl essence #WA424
- Bright silver #WA110
- Shimmering blue iridescence #WA440
- Shimmering green iridescence #WA441
- Shimmering gold iridescence #WA442
- Shimmering red iridescence #WA443
- Shimmering violet iridescence #WA444

One ounce bottles are adequate in all colors. I suggest the Polytranspar make your own medium kit which will save you money on colors.

Before spraying fish, remove pectoral and ventral fins.

The first color—Polytranspar superhide white #WA10—is applied to the lower half of the entire fish.

Next, supply Polytranspar yellow ochre #WA141 lightly to the top 3/4 of the fish. Use the larger head and needle in your airbrush for these first colors. Blend onto lower sides and underside beside anal fin. Apply first to upper half of fish (FIG. 6-25) and proceed downward under tail and lower sides.

Next, spraying from the top of the head downward, applying Polytranspar light bass green #WA60. This color is applied very lightly to the top 2/3 of the fish and entire caudal fin (COLOR SECTION, p. 6).

Then, lightly spray Polytranspar yellow gold pearl #WA425 to the lower sides of the fish.

Next, using the fine airbrush tip, lightly spray the discharge vent and the center of the underside of the jaw and the base of the ventral

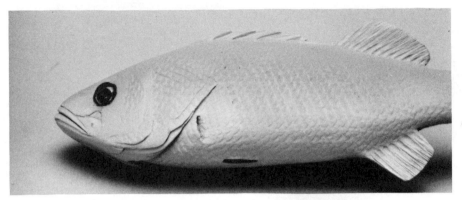

6-25   Yellow ochre applied to upper ³/₄ of fish.

fins and adjoining muscles with gill red (cadmium) #WA160. Then, still using the fine airbrush tip, blend in flesh #WA165 onto these areas to tone the red (FIGS. 6-26 and 6-27).

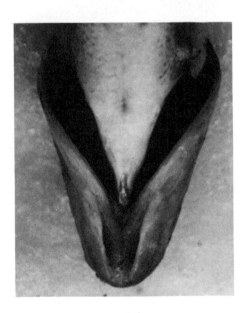

6-26   Lower jaw colors on perch.

Next, spray Polytranspar medium bass green #WA61 to the upper ²/₃ of the fish. This color is applied lightly, sprayed from the tail toward the head, using the fine head and needle in your airbrush. Only the back edges of the scales should be painted with this color (FIG. 6-28).

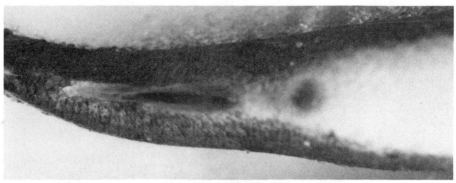

6-27 Discharge vent of actual perch.

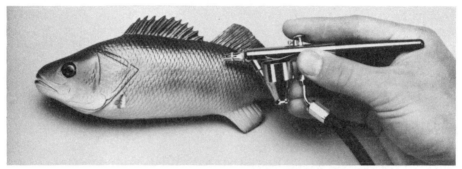

6-28 Medium bass green applied to back of scales.

Then, lightly mist entire fish with Polytranspar gold transparent toner #WA360. This will help blend the colors together.

The stripes are now sprayed in, using the fine airbrush tip. These stripes are applied by spraying the back half of each scale, periodically skipping scales as you move lower on the body. Random scales between stripes are also painted in this manner (COLOR SECTION, p. 6).

At this time, the pectoral and ventral fins should be painted. Spray the pectoral fins with Polytranspar yellow ochre #WA141. Then, spray the tips and edges with medium bass green #WA61. The lower edge of the pectoral fins are misted with superhide white #WA10. (Refer to figures of real fish.)

Spray the ventral fins with Polytranspar bright orange #WA90 and let dry completely. Then, apply superhide white #WA10. While still wet, carefully wipe off white paint from fin rays. This will leave the white paint between rays.

At this time, the ventral fins may be glued into place.

Use the same procedure for painting the anal fin as the pectoral fins. Then, spray the front of the anal fin with medium bass green #WA61 (FIG. 6-29).

6-29   Front of anal fin is sprayed with medium bass green.

Then, come back and spray the pectoral fins with Polytranspar sienna #WA200. While still wet, carefully wipe all sienna off of the fin rays. The sienna color will remain between the rays for a transparent look.

Next, glue the pectoral fins into place, and use sienna to touch-up where fins attach to the body.

The caudal and adipose fins may also be sprayed with sienna #WA200 and wiped while wet; again, leaving sienna between rays (COLOR SECTION, p. 6).

Next, touch up all areas where unwanted overspray has occurred.

When colors are all touched-up and correct, remove masking tape from the eyes. Then spray numerous coats of Polytranspar clear until desired wet look is achieved. The perch is then complete and ready for mounting.

Constructing the base

To paint the scenes or bases, I use Badger opaque airbrush paints. Liquitex paints may also be applied by brush.

I suggest going to an art supply store and selecting a wide variety of different colors for the scenes.

Painting scenes or bases requires the same type of reference work as painting fish. When duplicating rocks, driftwood, or any underwater objects, you must collect these objects, make them wet, and then attempt to duplicate the colors.

One painting tip for rocks is not to be too particular. A good way to paint rocks is to apply base coats, then splatter other colors onto the rocks with a large paintbrush. This is done as if you were removing extra water from a brush after cleaning (FIG. 6-30).

6-30 Splatter rocks with large paintbrush.

When attaching fish to the rocks or other objects, I make my own hardwood dowels. Hardwood dowels, such as cherry, provide much more strength on delicate carvings.

To make your own dowels, cut thin, square strips with a coping saw or band saw. Next, turn these strips until rounded to the proper shape and diameter on your disc belt sander (FIG. 6-31). When inserting dowels, drill small holes with your moto-tool and small bit as a guide hole to prevent spin-off with the drill bits.

Ideas on composition and balance will be discussed in the following chapter.

6-31 Cut dowels with disc belt sander.

Mounting the Fish

CHAPTER 7

Although this is the last chapter in the book, it is probably the most important. As more carvers begin fish carving, more competitions include fish categories, and more and more collectors of fine artwork continue buying wildlife wood carvings, only a select few fish carvers will be recognized as artists. The reason is that a carving is a carving until it takes on that extra little dimension. That extra dimension is composition.

Composition

To develop a good composition, a carver must be able to tell a story or set a mood—or both. Although it would take an entire book to teach methods of composition, style, design, and other artistic concepts, I will show a few examples of how carvings can be composed into simple wall hangings or ornate compositions, such as the musky carving entitled "Ambush" (COLOR SECTION, p.8).

Many times simple, passive carvings can be very beautiful compositions. It is not always necessary to create an exotic or elaborate wildlife scene. Some of my favorite pieces are small, basic pieces. Although these pieces are small and fairly simple, such as the trout carving (ON THE COVER), they will have flow and balance.

It is very important that when a fish is carved, the movements of one part of the fish correspond to the movements in other parts of the fish. As the movements within the fish must correspond, so must the fish and mount correspond. Carvings with these features will have flow and will be balanced.

To achieve flow in a carving, try to make the observer's eyes move with the fish, view the entire piece, and then return to the primary part of the piece. Flow can be seen in the smallmouth bass carving on the cover. The bass catches your eye, then your attention moves around the fish onto the crayfish. Since the crayfish is setting on the rock or lake bottom, your eyes should then be drawn back along the rocks toward the tail of the fish.

A balanced carving will have equal amounts of sculpture on either side of the center. This balance must be present when viewing from any direction. Balance in a carving can be seen in the perch scene. A triangle can be depicted by putting lines along the base, up the anchor rope, then back down to the base (FIG. 7-1). When attempting to balance this piece in its design stages, I chose to bring the anchor rope back to center by suspending the top perch over the base (FIG. 7-2). Also notice that the carving doesn't appear top or bottom heavy when complete (FIG. 7-3). Figure 7-4 shows the carving, entitled ''Jackpot.''

7-1   Lines in the triangle.

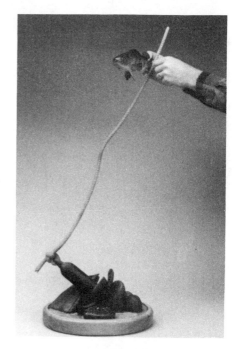

7-2   Balancing the triangle.

7-3   Perch attached by small dowels.

7-4 Fish swimming and hovering in random directions.

The perch on the cover of this book would be a much more simple way to display a carved perch.

Another good way to add interest and excitement, yet keep a carving very simple, is to select a unique piece of driftwood. The driftwood in this bluegill mount makes the piece very pleasing (COLOR SECTION, p. 2).

People seem to enjoy a lot of action in fish carvings. One way to convey a lot of action is to have the fish in feeding positions. A few examples of fish feeding are shown in the walleye and bass carvings.

The first feeding activity is illustrated in the trio of walleyes. One walleye has already overcome his prey, and the others are in hot pursuit. The carving is entitled "Feeding Frenzy" (COLOR SECTION, p. 3).

Another example of feeding activity is portrayed with the largemouth bass. The bass explodes toward the surface to consume the frog that is unaware of his approach. The carving is entitled "Frog Legs" (COLOR SECTION, p. 1).

The third example of feeding fish is the largemouth bass confronting a crayfish. The piece is entitled "Final Battle" (COLOR SECTION, p. 2); and the vegetation is used for balance.

"Final Battle" also shows another impressive way to display and compose fish carvings. This is by using an aquarium-type design.

My aquarium designs incorporate the use of cherry-framed glass to add a classy protective covering to some ornate pieces.

Another example of an aquarium scene is the tropical fish aquarium entitled "Tropical Delight" (COLOR SECTION, p. 5). When carving aquarium scenes, I try to make the scene active and pleasing from all sides.

Another excellent use of fish carving is to use the fish to accent bird carvings, such as the perch in the carving of a common loon (FIG. 7-5).

7-5 Perch as prey for the common loon.

One piece that combines balance, flow, and feeding activity within an aquarium scene is the aforementioned "Ambush" which won the 1987 World Wildlife Festival in group fish carving and in fish sculpture. This piece, carved entirely of cherry, exemplifies a muskellunge feeding in its natural habitat. As this 53-inch, 40-some pound musky explodes, it brings with it turbulent water, bending and breaking vegetation. The 27-inch northern pike's life is ended quickly as his role changes from predator to prey within an instant. And as the perch swim away in nervous relief, a crayfish and bluegill hide from numerous troubles (COLOR SECTION, p. 8).

S u p p l i e r s

BADGER AIR-BRUSH CO.
9128 W. Belmont Avenue
Franklin Park, Illinois   60131

R.J. BEYER GALLERIES
1115 N. Main Street
Racine, Wisconsin   53402

CURT'S WATERFOWL CORNER
Box 228
123 Leboeuf Street
Montegut, Louisiana   70377

DREMEL
P.O. Box 1468
Racine, Wisconsin   53401

VAN DYKE'S
P.O. Box 278
Woonsocket, South Dakota   57385

WILDLIFE ARTIST SUPPLY CO.
P.O. Box 967
Monroe, Georgia   30655

WOODCRAFTERS SUPPLY
3701 Durand Avenue
Racine, Wisconsin   53405

INDEX